Dig, Sid, Dig!

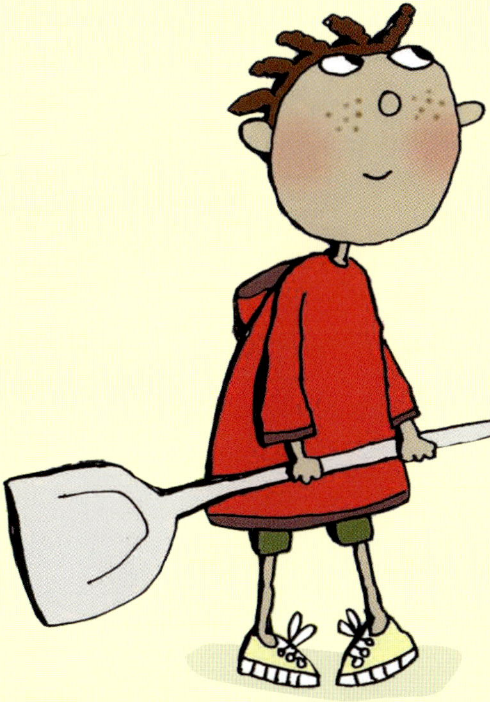

Written by Jeanne Willis
Illustrated by Jess Mikhail

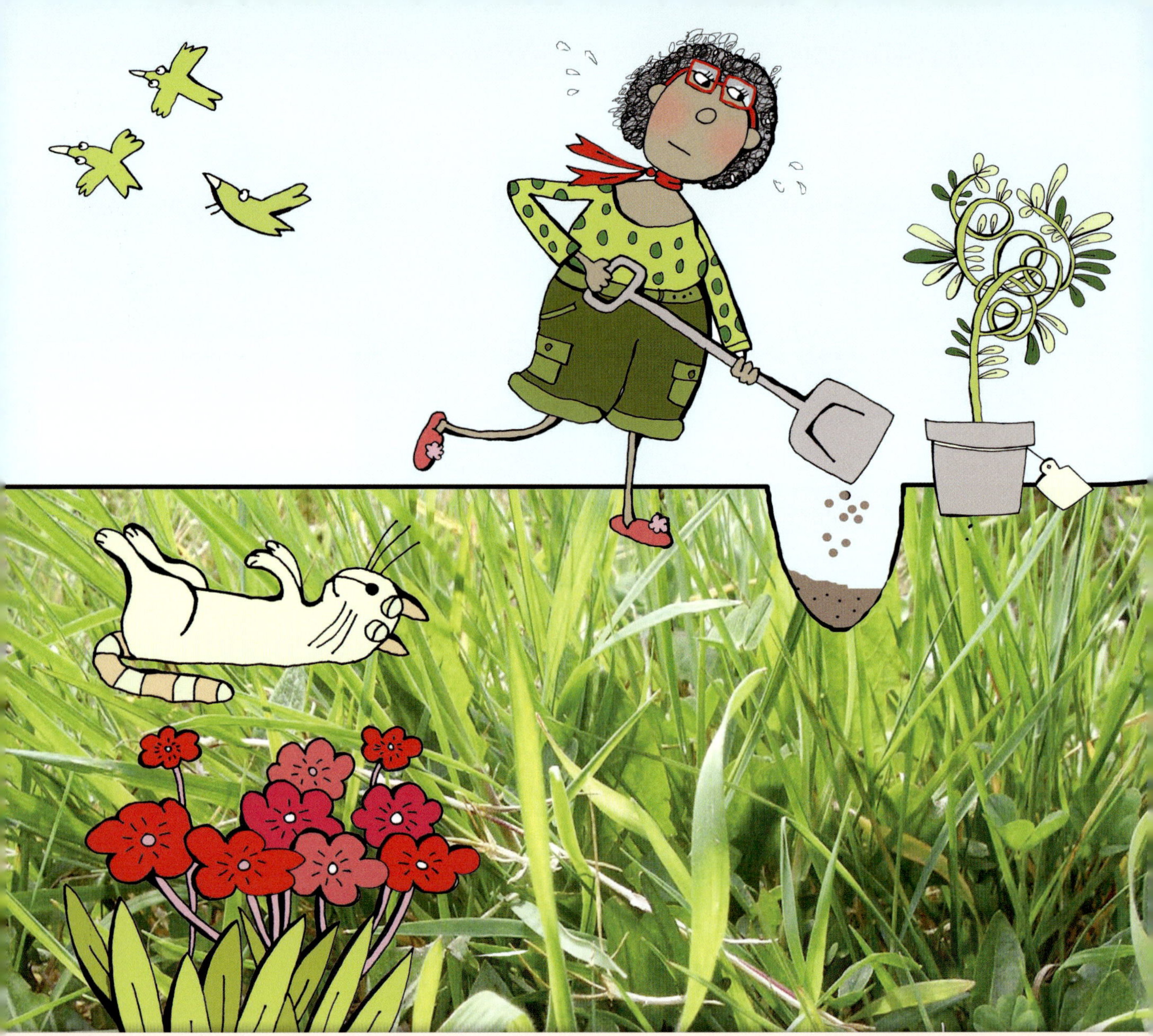

Nan digs and digs.

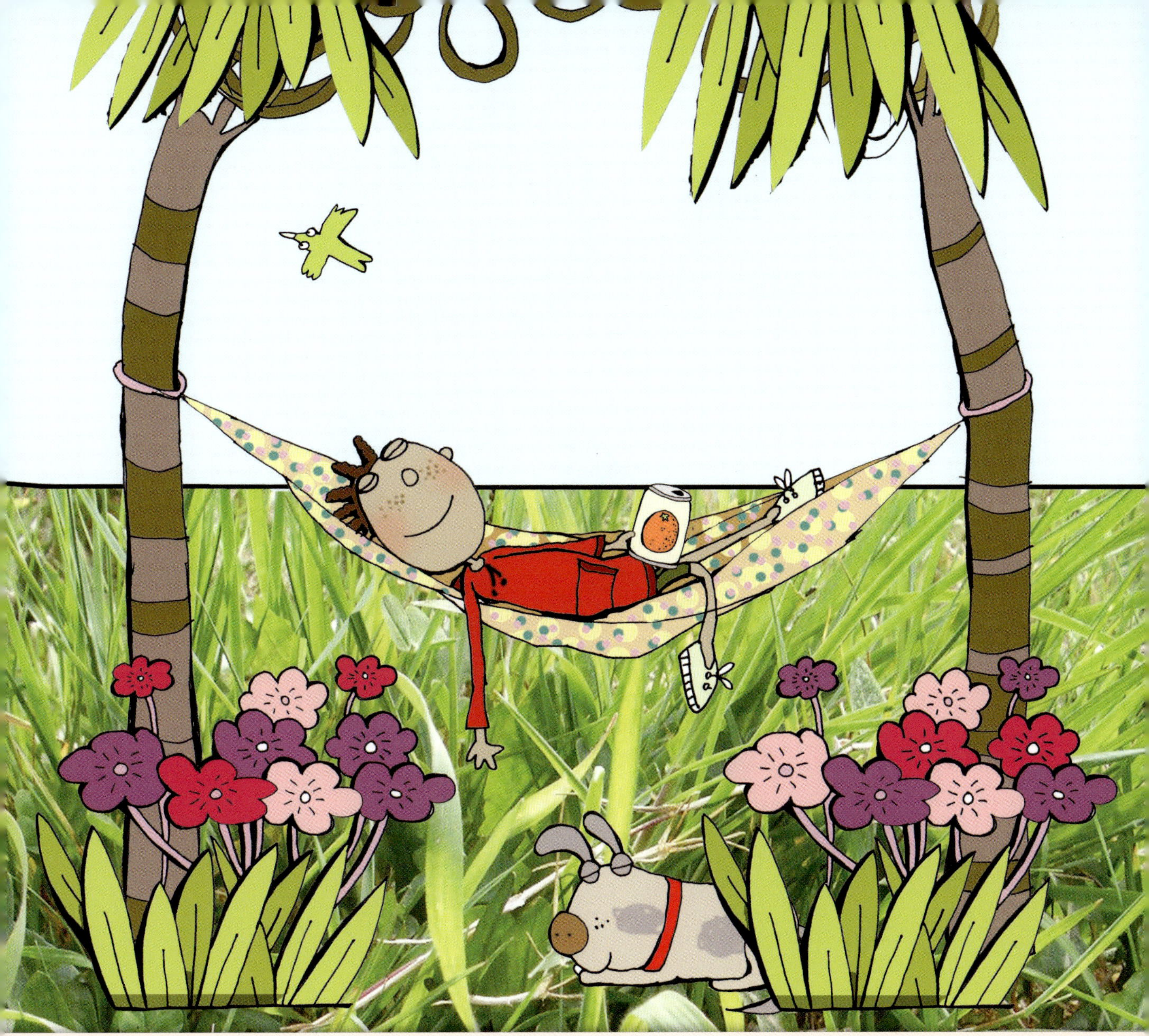

Sid sips pop.

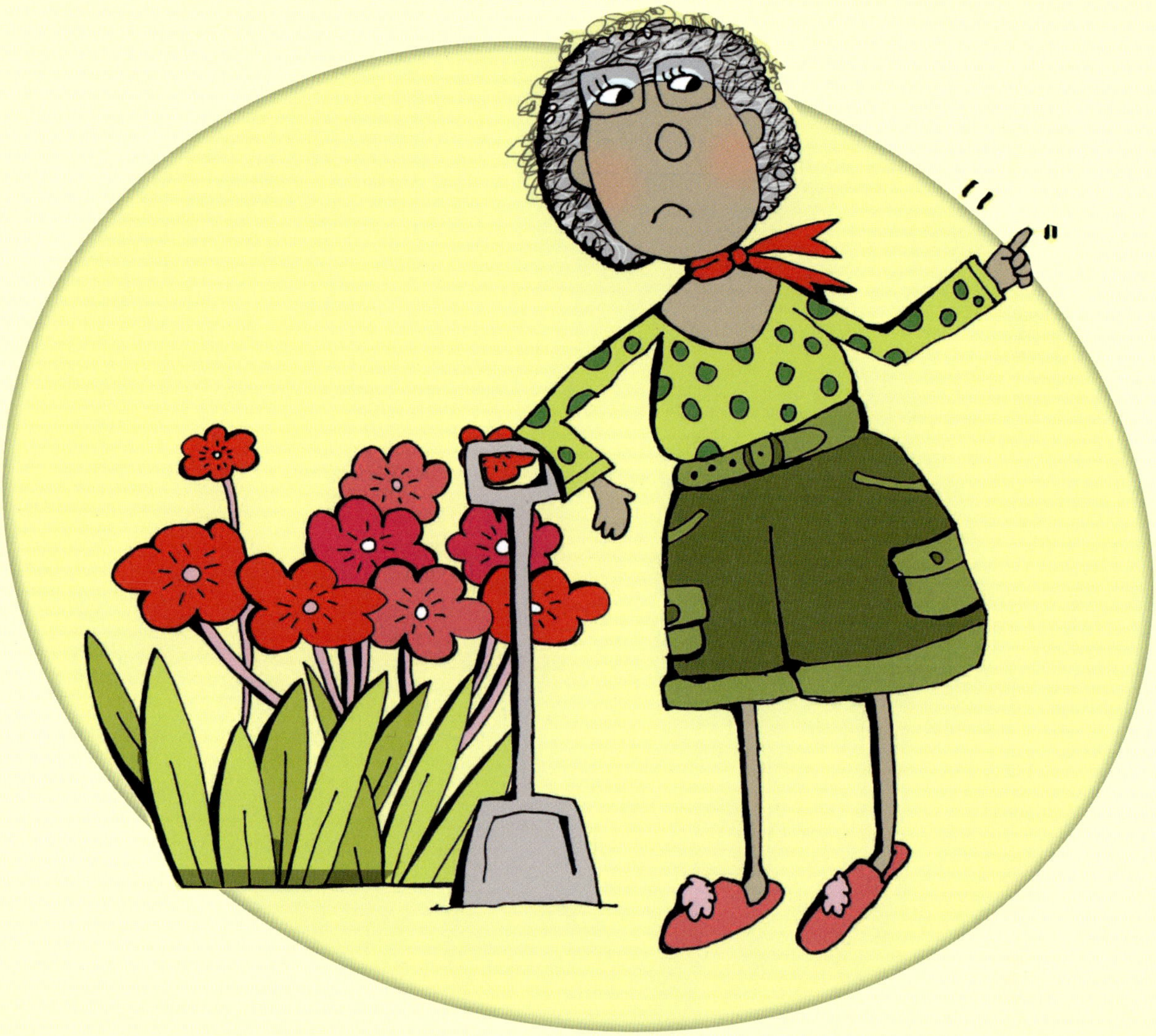

Nan nags and nags.

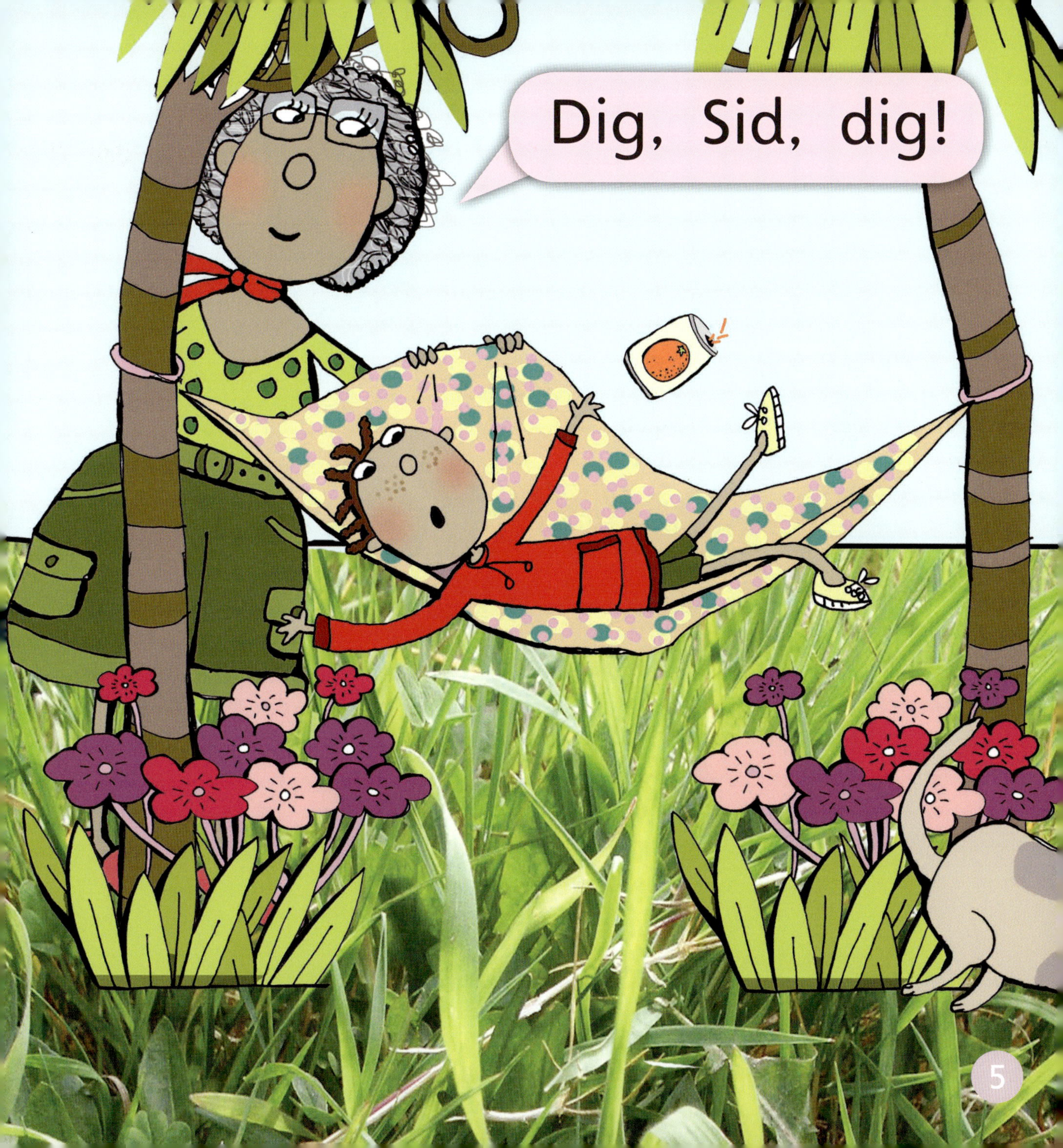
Dig, Sid, dig!

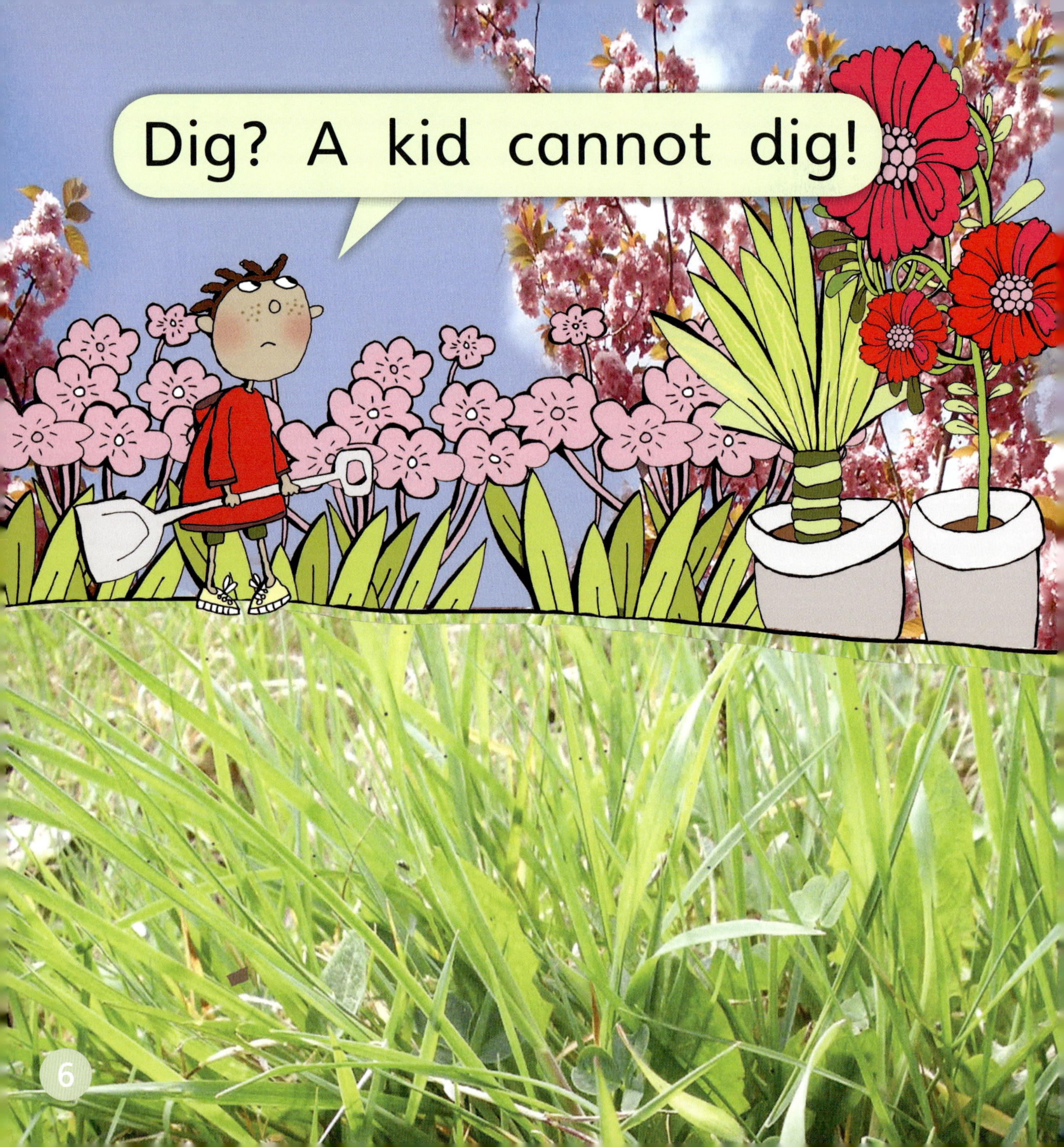
Dig? A kid cannot dig!

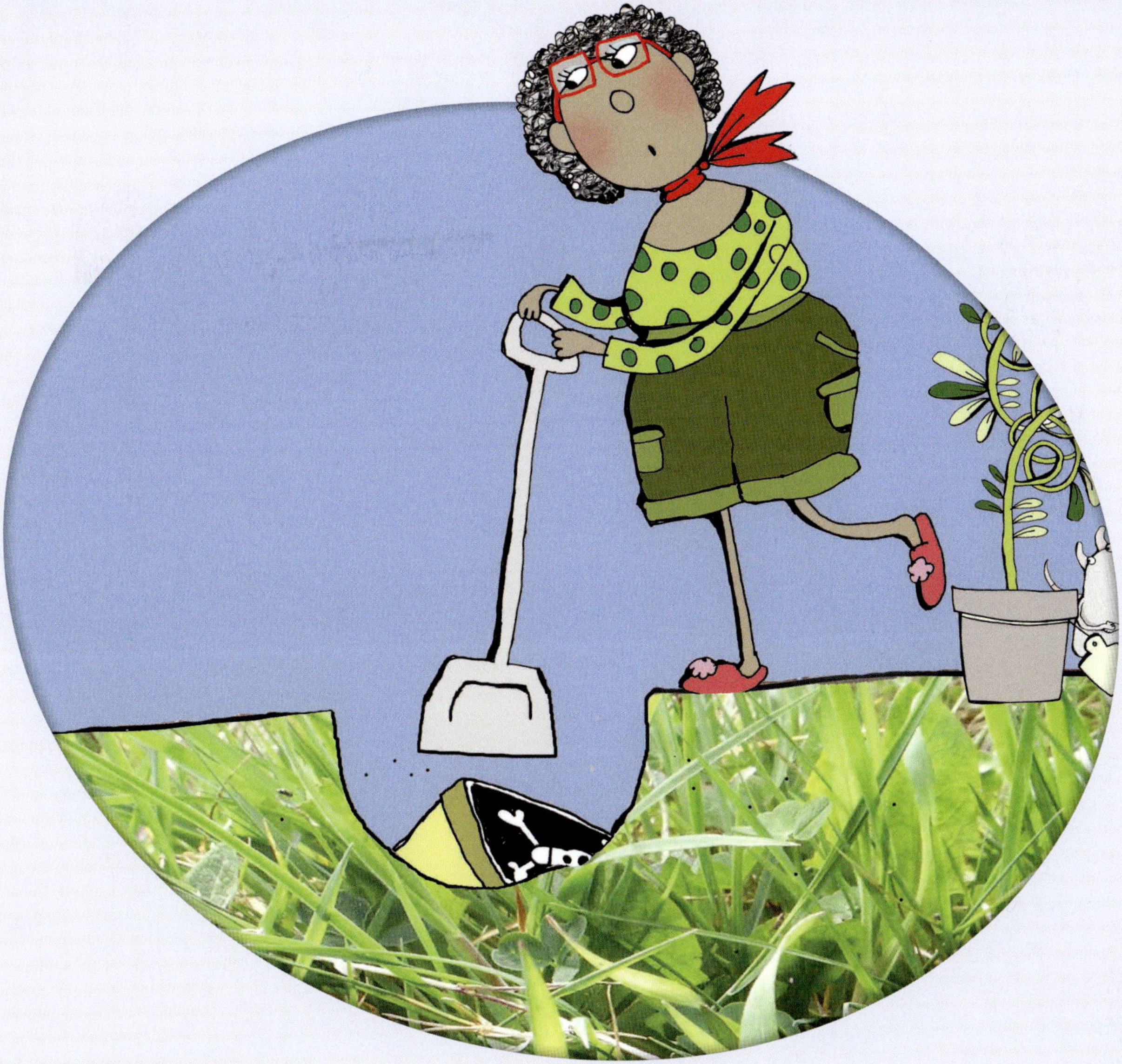

Nan taps a tin.

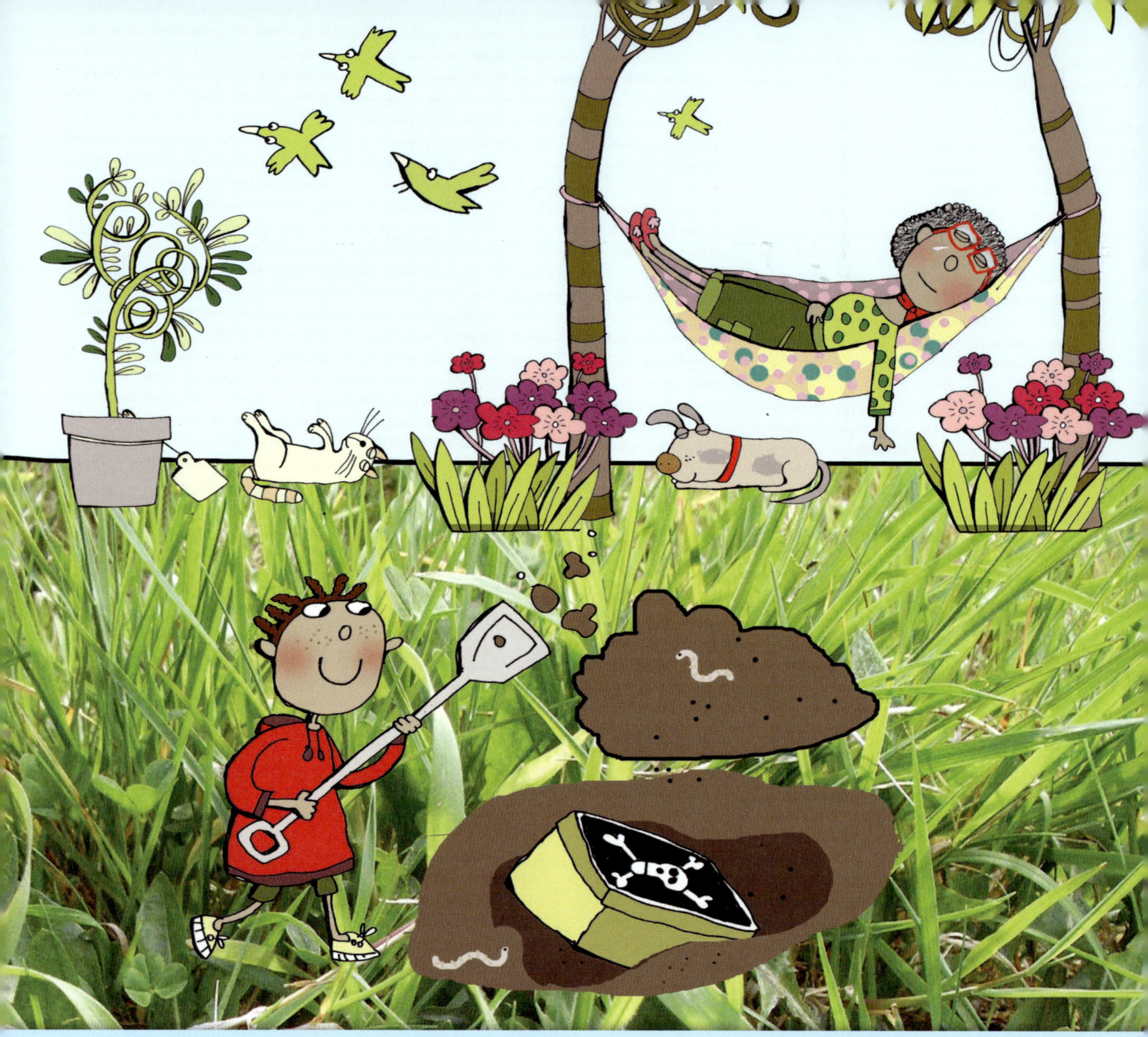

Nan got Sid to dig!